# Andrew Luck

By Jon M. Fishman

AMAZING
ATHLETES

Lerner Publications Company • Minneapolis

Lerner Publications Company
A division of Lerner Publishing Group, Inc.
241 First Avenue North
Minneapolis, MN 55401 U.S.A.

Website address: www.lernerbooks.com


Library of Congress Cataloging-in-Publication Data

Fishman, Jon M.
    Andrew Luck / by Jon M. Fishman.
      pages  cm — (Amazing Athletes)
    Includes index.
    ISBN 978–1–4677–1879–0 (lib. bdg. : alk. paper)
    ISBN 978–1–4677–1889–9 (eBook)
    1. Luck, Andrew, 1989—Juvenile literature. 2. Football players—United States—Biography—Juvenile literature. 3. Quarterbacks (Football)—United States—Biography—Juvenile literature.
I. Title.
GV939.B685F57 2014
796.332092—dc23 [B]                                2013000591

Manufactured in the United States of America
1 – BP – 7/15/13

# TABLE OF CONTENTS

Andrew Luck throws a pass during a game against the Detroit Lions.

# LAST-SECOND WIN

Indianapolis Colts **quarterback** Andrew Luck threw the football high and deep. It soared down the left side of the field. **Wide receiver** LaVon Brazill raised his hands above his head to catch the ball. Touchdown!

The Colts were playing against the Detroit Lions on December 2, 2012. Detroit had the lead, 33–28. The Lions had been ahead for most of the game. Andrew's touchdown pass to Brazill made it close.  But there were fewer than three minutes left in the fourth quarter. Would the Colts have time to score another touchdown?

Andrew *(second from left)* and his teammates line up for the next play.

Detroit had the ball. They hoped to keep it until the end of the game. The Lions didn't want to give Andrew and the Colts another chance to score.

Detroit **running back** Mikel Leshoure ran with the ball. But he was crushed by Indianapolis **defenders** after just one yard. It was fourth down. The Lions decided to **punt**.

Andrew and the Colts took control of the ball. There was only one minute and seven seconds left in the game. They had to go 75 yards to score a touchdown. Andrew ran with the ball for nine yards. Then he threw a pass to Reggie Wayne for 26 yards.

The Colts were driving down the field. Soon, Andrew had his team all the way to the Lions' 12-yard line. He took the ball with eight seconds left on the clock. Andrew stepped forward. He hit Donnie Avery with a short pass. Avery ran the ball across the **goal line** for a touchdown. There was no time left on the clock. Indianapolis won the game!

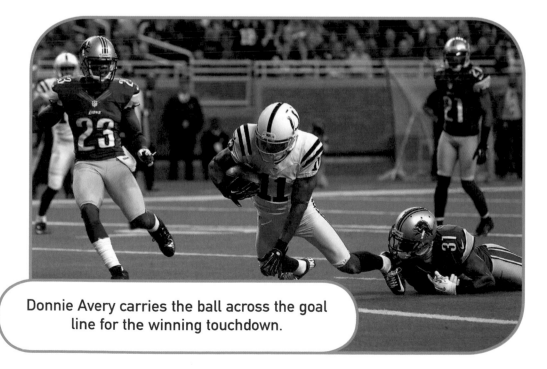

Donnie Avery carries the ball across the goal line for the winning touchdown.

Andrew *(left)* celebrates the victory with LaVon Brazill *(center)* and Dwayne Allen *(right)*.

Indianapolis coach Bruce Arians knows his team is special. They have a chance to win every game with Andrew leading the way. "Some teams find ways to win," Coach Arians said. "Others don't."

Andrew *(left)* in a 2011 photo with his family

# FAMILY TIME

Andrew Austen Luck was born on September 12, 1989. He has two sisters named Mary Ellen and Emily. He has a brother named Addison. Their parents, Oliver and Kathy, are both lawyers. Oliver played quarterback for the National Football League's (NFL) Houston Oilers for three seasons. The Oilers later became the Tennessee Titans.

Andrew was born in Washington, D.C. But Oliver and Kathy moved the family to Frankfurt, Germany, in 1990. Oliver had a new job. He became **general manager** of the Frankfurt Galaxy.

The World League of American Football later changed its name to NFL Europe. The league was canceled in 2007.

The Galaxy were a team in the World League of American Football.

The family moved to London, England, in 1996. Andrew saw famous buildings all over Europe. The Lucks didn't watch much TV. Instead, the family played games

Andrew liked football even as a little boy.

Austin is one of the biggest cities in Texas.

such as Scrabble. But Andrew's sister Mary Ellen usually won. "She's a lot smarter than me," Andrew said. He also played soccer. But American football isn't popular in England.

Oliver left his job with the World League in 2000. The Lucks moved to Austin, Texas. Eleven-year-old Andrew had never played a real football game. It was time he gave the sport a try. Andrew joined the Lake Travis Wildcats youth team. He played as a defender and a running back.

Before long, Andrew was playing quarterback. "My dad had taught me how to throw," Andrew said. "He was my sports hero at a young age, so I guess I could throw a little better than the other kids."

The family moved again when Oliver took a new job. This time, they settled in Houston, Texas. Andrew entered Stratford High School as a freshman in 2004. High school football is a big deal in Texas. Andrew set out to show that he could play with anyone.

Andrew played football at Stratford High School.

Andrew has always had a strong throwing arm.

# TEXAS STAR

Stratford High School football coach Eliot Allen had heard a lot about Andrew. "We thought he would be good," Allen said. "But we've also had some kids whose parents were NFL guys and they couldn't play. You just never know what to expect."

Andrew worked hard to get ready for the 2005 season.

Andrew played quarterback for the freshman team in 2004. But his season was cut short when he broke a bone near his shoulder.

The broken bone healed. Andrew got ready for the 2005 season. He has always worked hard at practice. It's a lesson he learned from his father. Oliver taught Andrew to play with heart and to respect the game. "The message got across," Andrew said.

Andrew was named the starting quarterback of the **varsity** team in 2005. It's rare for a sophomore to earn such an important job. He had a good season, throwing for 1,529 yards. He also threw seven touchdowns. Andrew was even better in 2006. He passed for 2,926 yards with 27 touchdowns.

The young quarterback was starting to get attention from college **scouts**. People all around the country were talking about Andrew.

Andrew's football skills attracted the attention of college scouts.

They talked even more when he threw for 2,684 yards and 19 touchdowns as a senior in 2007.

It was time for Andrew to choose a college. Many schools offered him **scholarships**. Andrew wasn't just a star quarterback. He was also a good student. He had earned mostly As during high school.

Andrew remembered the beautiful buildings he'd seen while living in Europe. He decided to study to become

Andrew wanted to study architecture. He had seen buildings such as this shopping center when he lived in Frankfurt, Germany.

an **architect**. Stanford University in California has a good football team. NFL greats such as John Elway had gone to Stanford. It is also a good place to learn to be an architect.

Stanford also had one other thing in its favor. Jim Harbaugh was the head coach of the football team. Harbaugh had played 14 seasons as a quarterback in the NFL. Andrew thought he could learn a lot from Harbaugh.

Andrew *(with the ball)* didn't get on the field during a game at Stanford until his second year.

# STANFORD STANDOUT

Andrew announced that he was going to Stanford. He was happy with the choice. "It's an honor to be able to put on a jersey and say, 'I'm a Stanford quarterback,'" Andrew said. "I love saying it."

Andrew began his college career as a redshirt freshman. This meant that he wouldn't play in games in 2008. Instead, he would learn about life in college. He would practice and get stronger. Being a redshirt freshman also meant that the year didn't count. He would still be able to play four seasons for Stanford if he wished.

Stanford began the 2009 season with Andrew at quarterback. It was a fine year. With Andrew leading the way, the team scored 434 points.

Andrew looks to make a pass in a game against San Jose State University.

Stanford football fans celebrate with the team at a home game.

This was the highest point total ever for Stanford football. They finished with eight wins and five losses.

Stanford faced the University of Oklahoma in the 2009 Sun Bowl. But Andrew had hurt his finger in a game against the University of Notre Dame. He couldn't play in the Sun Bowl. Oklahoma won, 31–27.

In 2010, Andrew had 32 touchdown passes. He threw only eight **interceptions** all year. Stanford beat Virginia Tech University in the Orange Bowl, 40–12. Andrew threw four touchdowns in the game. "It's a wonderful way to cap off the season," he said.

By now, people were talking about Andrew's future in the NFL. Most scouts agreed that he would be the first player taken in the 2011 **draft**. But Andrew decided to return to Stanford for another year. He wanted to earn his **degree**.

Andrew celebrates winning the Orange Bowl with his teammates.

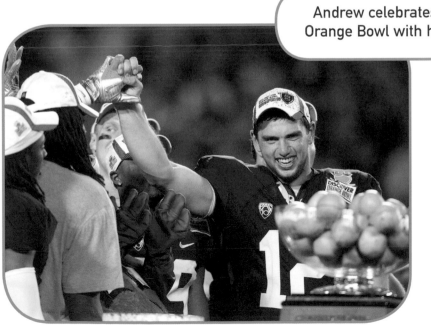

Andrew's father agreed with his son's decision. "It's not like the NFL is going anywhere; it's one of the best-run leagues in the world," Oliver said. "It will still be there when he graduates."

Coach Harbaugh had also been getting attention from the NFL. But unlike Andrew, Harbaugh decided not to wait. The coach announced after the Orange Bowl that he was leaving Stanford. He became the head coach of the San Francisco 49ers.

Andrew was at the top of his game during the 2011 season.

# "A FOOTBALL DREAM COME TRUE"

Life at Stanford was different without Coach Harbaugh. But Andrew's play on the field was as good as ever. He threw 37 touchdown passes in 2011. This was the most of his career. It was also a new Stanford record.

Andrew and Stanford played against Oklahoma State University in the Fiesta Bowl. Oklahoma State came out on top, 41–38. Andrew played well. But it wasn't enough. "In the end, we lost, and I'm as much to blame as anyone," he said after the game.

It was still a great year for Andrew. The star quarterback finished second in voting for the Heisman Trophy. The Heisman is given each year to college football's most outstanding player. Baylor University's Robert Griffin III took the award home.

Andrew tries to make a play against Oklahoma State in the Fiesta Bowl.

After four years at Stanford, Andrew had earned his architecture degree. It was time to move to the NFL. The Indianapolis Colts had the first pick in the 2012 draft. Most people thought the Colts would take Andrew. But some thought they would choose Griffin instead.

Andrew *(right)* holds up his new Colts jersey after being chosen in the 2012 draft.

The Colts made Andrew the first pick on April 26, 2012. The Washington Redskins chose Griffin with the second pick.

Peyton Manning has been named the NFL's Most Valuable Player (MVP) four times. No other player has won the award this many times.

Andrew would have to work hard with his new team. People expected him to play well right away. The Colts had released long-time quarterback Peyton Manning, who signed with the Denver Broncos. Manning had been with Indianapolis since 1998. He led the team to victory in the Super Bowl in 2007.

Peyton Manning throws a pass against the New York Giants.

"You don't really replace a guy like that," Andrew said. "You can't. You just try to do the best you can."

The Colts were sure that Andrew's best would be good enough. They signed the young thrower to a **contract** worth $22.1 million. Andrew was rich!

Andrew helped make the Colts a winning team in 2012. They won 11 games and made the **playoffs**. But they lost to the Baltimore Ravens in the first round. Baltimore went on to win the Super Bowl.

Andrew warms up before the opening game of the 2012 season.

Andrew has a bright future in the NFL.

Indianapolis fans will never forget Peyton Manning. But Andrew and his teammates are ready to make new memories. "If one day I can be mentioned alongside Peyton as one of the football greats, that would be a football dream come true," he said. Andrew has the skills to make that football dream a reality.

# Selected Career Highlights

**2012** Chosen by the Indianapolis Colts with the first pick in the draft
Began season as Colts starting quarterback

**2011** Named Pac 12 Conference Offensive Player of the Year for the second time
Finished second in Heisman Trophy voting behind Robert Griffin III
Led Stanford to a 11–2 record

**2010** Named Pac 12 Conference Offensive Player of the Year
Finished second in voting for the Heisman Trophy behind Cam Newton
Set Stanford record with 32 touchdown passes in a season

**2009** Named National Freshman of the Year by Scout.com
Led Stanford to most points scored in a season

**2008** Did not play in games as redshirt freshman
Graduated high school as the co-valedictorian of his class

**2007** Ranked the fourth-best high school quarterback in the United States by Scout.com
Passed for 2,684 yards and 19 touchdowns as a high school senior

**2006** Passed for 2,926 yards and 27 touchdowns as a high school junior

**2005** Named starting quarterback at Stratford High School in Houston, Texas
Passed for 1,529 yards and seven touchdowns as a high school sophomore

# Glossary

**architect:** a person who designs buildings

**contract:** a deal signed by a player and a team that states the amount of money the player is paid and the number of years he plays

**defenders:** football players whose job it is to stop the other team from scoring points

**degree:** a piece of paper declaring that a person has successfully completed school

**draft:** a yearly event in which teams take turns choosing new players from a group

**general manager:** the person who makes decisions about players for a sports team

**goal line:** a line that appears at both ends of a football field. The ball must cross the goal line to score a touchdown.

**interceptions:** passes that are caught by players on the other team. An interception results in the opposing team getting control of the ball.

**playoffs:** a series of games played to decide the league's championship team

**punt:** to kick the ball after it is dropped before it hits the ground. A punt results in the opposing team getting control of the ball.

**quarterback:** a player whose main job is to throw passes

**running back:** a football player whose main job is to run with the ball

**scholarships:** money awarded to students to help pay college tuition

**scouts:** football experts who watch players closely to judge their ability

**varsity:** the top sports team at a school

**wide receiver:** a football player whose main job is to catch passes

# Further Reading & Websites

Fishman, Jon M. *Robert Griffin III*. Minneapolis: Lerner Publications Company, 2014.

Kennedy, Mike, and Mark Stewart. *Touchdown: The Power and Precision of Football's Perfect Play*. Minneapolis: Millbrook Press, 2010.

Savage, Jeff. *Peyton Manning*. Minneapolis: Lerner Publications Company, 2007.

*Indianapolis Colts: The Official Site*
http://www.colts.com
The official website of the Indianapolis Colts includes the team schedule and game results, late-breaking news, team history, biographies of players like Andrew Luck, and much more.

*The Official Site of the National Football League*
http://www.nfl.com
The NFL's official website provides fans with the latest scores, schedules, and standings, biographies and statistics of players, as well as the league's official online store.

*Sports Illustrated Kids*
http://www.sikids.com
The *Sports Illustrated Kids* website covers all sports, including the NFL.

# Index

# Photo Acknowledgments

The images in this book are used with the permission of: © Mark Cunningham/Detroit Lions/Getty Images, pp. 4, 29; AP Photo/Paul Sancya, p. 5; © Dave Reginek/Getty Images, p. 7; AP Photo/Rick Osentoski, p. 8; Courtesy of Kathy Luck, pp. 9, 10; © Brandon Seidel/Dreamstime.com, p. 11; AP Photo/Aaron M. Sprecher, pp. 12, 13; AP Photo/Margaret Bowles, pp. 14, 15; © Mircea Nicolescu/Dreamstime.com, p. 16; © Mike Ehrmann/ Getty Images, p. 18; © Ezra Shaw/Getty Images, p. 19; © Jason O. Watson/ Getty Images, p. 20; © Joel Auerbach/Getty Images, p. 21; © Rob Tringali/ SportsChrome/Getty Images, pp. 23, 24; © Al Bello/Getty Images, p. 25; © Jonathan Daniel/Getty Images, p. 27; © Andy Lyons/Getty Images, p. 29.

Front Cover: © Peter G. Aiken/Getty Images.

Main body text set in Caecilia LT Std 55 Roman 16/28.
Typeface provided by Adobe Systems.